WILDLIFE
AT RISK

TURTLES AND TORTOISES

Vassili Papastavrou

The Bookwright Press
New York · 1992

WILDLIFE AT RISK

Bears
Birds of Prey
Elephants
Gorillas
Monkeys
Pandas
Rhinos
Seals and Sea Lions
Tigers
Turtles and Tortoises
Whales and Dolphins
Wolves

Cover: A leopard tortoise crossing a track in Moremi National Park, Botswana.

First published in the
United States in 1992 by
The Bookwright Press
387 Park Avenue South
New York, NY 10016

First published in 1991 by
Wayland (Publishers) Ltd
61 Western Road, Hove
East Sussex BN3 1JD, England

Library of Congress Cataloging-in-Publication Data

Papastavrou, Vassili.
  Turtles and tortoises / by Vassili Papastavrou.
    p. cm. — (Wildlife at risk)
  Includes bibliographical references and index.
  Summary: Introduces the different species of turtles and tortoises, their habits, and habitats, and discusses their endangered status and current conservation efforts.
  ISBN 0-531-18453-6
  1. Turtles — Juvenile literature. 2. Endangered species — Juvenile literature. 3. Wildlife conservation — Juvenile literature.
  [1. Turtles. 2. Rare animals. 3. Wildlife conservation.]
  I. Title II. Series.
QL666.C5P37   1992
597.92— dc20   91-20098
                                         CIP
                                          AC

Typeset by Kalligraphic Design Ltd
Printed in Italy by L.E.G.O. S.p.A

Contents

What are turtles and tortoises? . . 4

Sea turtles 8

Terrapins and freshwater turtles . . 12

Giant tortoises 14

Chelonians at risk 16

Saving turtles and tortoises . . . 24

Glossary 30

Further reading 31

Useful addresses 31

Index 32

All words printed in **bold** are explained
in the glossary on page 30.

WHAT ARE TURTLES AND TORTOISES?

Turtles and tortoises belong to the group of animals known as **chelonia**. Most turtles are **aquatic** and have flipper limbs for swimming in water. Tortoises live on land and have stumpy front legs. Terrapins are also members of the group called chelonians. Most terrapins live in water.

Above *Like most chelonians, the desert tortoise has a hard shell.*

Left *Loggerhead turtles have powerful front flippers and can swim fast underwater.*

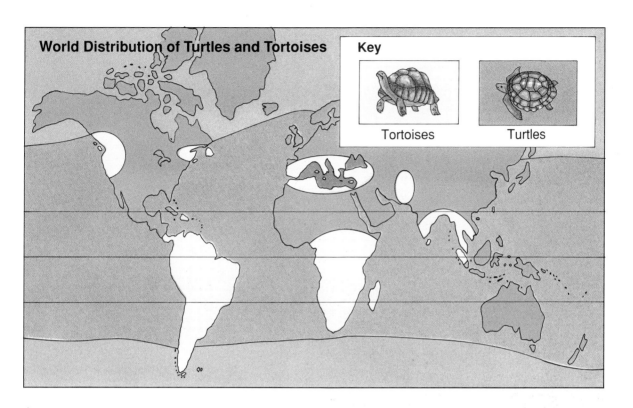

World Distribution of Turtles and Tortoises

Key

Tortoises

Turtles

All chelonians have shells that are usually hard. This is for protection. When they are frightened, most chelonians hide by pulling their legs and heads inside their shells. The shell is often heavy, so most chelonians move quite slowly. Some chelonians move faster. The pancake tortoise has a flat, light shell, so it is able to move quickly and hide under rocks. Sea turtles are **streamlined**, so they are able to swim fast. They have flatter shells, so they cannot hide their heads.

Most turtles and tortoises are found in warmer parts of the world. They are sensitive to heat and cold. If an animal becomes too cool, it will lie in the sun. However, chelonians can also get too hot. Desert tortoises stay underground during the hottest part of the day to avoid the sun. Sea turtles are usually found in warmer seas since they have to gain heat from the water.

This angulated tortoise lays several large eggs. While she lays them, she should not be disturbed.

There are over 250 **species** of chelonians. They live on the land, in rivers and in the sea. Male and female chelonians look similar, but the males usually have longer tails than females. The males sometimes have long claws on their front legs. The claws help some species hold onto the females during **mating**. When the females are ready to lay their eggs, they choose the site of their nests very carefully. Most produce a large number of eggs and do not look after them once they have been laid.

Hawksbill turtles can lay over two hundred eggs but some species lay far fewer. The pancake tortoise lays just one egg. If the eggs stay cool, more males are produced. If the eggs are warmer, then more females are produced.

Turtles and tortoises can live for a very long time.

A hatchling uses its egg tooth to break out of its shell. This is a young diamondback terrapin.

Galapagos giant tortoises have lived over a hundred years in **captivity**. The oldest tortoise in captivity was an Aldabran giant tortoise that was over 150 years old.

This book will describe only a few examples from the big group of chelonians. These are animals that have existed on earth since the time of the dinosaurs. But because of human activities, many species of chelonians are now at risk.

SEA TURTLES

There are seven species of sea turtles. The largest is the leatherback turtle, which can weigh 1,550 lb (700 kg), almost the weight of a small car. The smallest is the olive ridley, which weighs about 77 lb (35 kg). Six of these seven species are **endangered**. Kemp's ridley is the rarest sea turtle and nests on one beach in Mexico. In 1947 there were 40,000 of these turtles. Now there are fewer than 800 left.

A male loggerhead turtle mates with a female turtle in the water close to Australian nesting beaches.

Sea turtles spend most of their lives at sea and only come out of the water to nest. In the waters close to the nesting beaches, male turtles mate with the females. The females come onto the shore and scoop out a hole in the sand and lay about a hundred eggs. About two months later, the eggs **hatch** and the baby turtles (called hatchlings) make their way to the sea.

The female green turtle scoops out a hole in the sand on the shore and lays about a hundred eggs.

Below *The green turtle hatchlings have emerged from the nest and are making their way toward the water.*

After the hatchlings swim out to sea, no one is sure what happens to them. Scientists think that possibly the young turtles drift in rafts of seaweed with the ocean currents for the first year of their lives. We do not know how long it takes for a hatchling to grow into an adult turtle. It could take up to thirty years!

The female turtle usually returns to nest on the beach several times in one year. In this way she lays many eggs. However, very few eggs will ever develop into adult turtles. Crabs and foxes burrow into the nests and eat the eggs. Hatchlings are eaten by gulls and other sea birds as they make their way to the sea. Once in the sea, they become food for sharks and other fish.

A green turtle returns to the sea after successfully nesting on a beach in the Sultanate of Oman.

Turtles always seem to return to the same beach to nest. Scientists think that they go back to the beach where they were born. Many turtles make long **migrations** to nest. That is because nesting beaches are not always in the same place as feeding areas.

Leatherbacks make the longest migrations, to find the jellyfish they like to eat. Some animals travel over 3,700 miles (6,000 km). One turtle migrated from a beach in South America all the way across the Atlantic Ocean. Hawksbills do not need to make long journeys. The sea sponges and sea squirts they like to eat are found on **coral reefs**, and their nesting beaches are usually nearby.

Other sea turtles eat different foods. Loggerhead turtles have powerful jaws, which they use to eat crabs or to break open shells. Green turtles are **vegetarians** and eat only seaweed and seagrass.

A hawksbill turtle looking for food on a coral reef.

TERRAPINS AND FRESHWATER TURTLES

Terrapins belong to the family of aquatic turtles that live on land and in fresh water. Terrapins are found on all continents except for Australia. There are a great many species of terrapin and freshwater turtles. The diamondback terrapin inhabits salt marshes and coastal areas of the east coast of the United States.

The diamondback terrapin used to be eaten as a delicacy and almost died out.

Other terrapins inhabit rivers and ponds and areas of fresh water. Some freshwater turtles that belong to this family live on land.

Snake-necked turtles live in South America, Australia and New Guinea. This family of turtles have very long necks. One example is the mata mata turtle that lives in the Amazon River. Instead of chasing fish it waits for its prey and reaches out its long neck to catch it.

Box turtles have a very domed shell, which is hinged. This means that they can seal the openings at either end, which gives them good protection against attack.

Another group of freshwater turtles is the snapping turtles. These are found in parts of the United States. Snapping turtles have powerful jaws, which can cause injury to humans. The largest member of this family is the alligator snapping turtle. It lies still in the water and feeds by tricking fish or other food into its mouth before snapping them up.

Above *Only adult box turtles are able to shut their shells this way.*

Below *The alligator snapping turtle has powerful jaws to snap up its prey.*

GIANT TORTOISES

Some tortoises are very large and are called giant tortoises. The Seychelles and Mascarene Islands, which lie in the Indian Ocean, were once the home of very many giant tortoises. However they were hunted to **extinction** over two hundred years ago.

There are now very few giant tortoises left living on the Galapagos Islands.

Now the giant tortoises are found only in the Galapagos Islands (in the Pacific Ocean) and Aldabra Atoll (in the Indian Ocean).

There used to be fifteen slightly different kinds of giant tortoises that lived on the Galapagos Islands. Most lived on separate islands and became **adapted** to different ways of life. Four kinds are now extinct and many others have been reduced to low numbers because of human activities.

The giant tortoises are well adapted to the islands they live on. Some kinds of giant tortoises have shells that are raised at the front. This allows them to lift their heads and eat tall plants. Galapagos tortoises and finches also help each other. The tortoise sticks its neck out so that the bird can pick out and eat the **ticks** that suck tortoise blood. The Aldabran tortoises also suffer from animals that bite. But they wallow in the mud to get rid of mosquitoes instead.

Two giant tortoises coming out of a pool of water where they like to wallow in the mud.

CHELONIANS AT RISK

Tortoises in danger

Early seafarers who visited the Galapagos Islands over a hundred years ago used to take away the giant tortoises for food. In those days there were probably several hundred thousand giant tortoises. Now, fewer than 15,000 are alive. People have brought in pigs, dogs and rats, which dig up the tortoise eggs and eat them. Goats eat the plants that tortoises need to feed on.

Above *This boy lives on the Galapagos Islands. Islanders' livestock and pets have reduced the number of tortoises.*

In Morocco, the forest habitats of tortoises are being destroyed.

Many tortoises are killed or injured by motor vehicles. This tortoise was rescued, and later recovered.

Tortoises are suffering because of human activities and some are becoming very rare. In Morocco several species of tortoises live in thick forests. These forests are being destroyed and turned into grazing land. When an area is turned into farmland, tortoises are often crushed by farm machinery.

Even protected areas have been destroyed. In Greece a protected site for Hermann's tortoise has been turned into an area for vacation homes.

Another serious problem for tortoises is forest fire. All over southern Europe, tortoises are at risk from burning.

Until quite recently several kinds of tortoises such as Hermann's tortoise and the spur-thighed tortoise were imported into Britain and other countries as pets, but now this is no longer allowed.

Turtles in danger

Sea turtles are easy prey for hunters to catch because the turtles come on shore to lay their eggs. In Indonesia many green turtles are killed for food. Turtle eggs are also eaten in many parts of the world. Hawksbill turtles are caught by hunters, and their shells are used to make **"tortoiseshell"** ornaments.

In the sea, thousands of turtles are accidentally caught by fishermen. One problem is the use of drift nets. These nets catch not only fish but also turtles and other animals that get tangled up in the nets and drown.

In many parts of the world, turtles are killed by local people for food.

We do not know how many turtles die in this way. In the Gulf of Mexico, shrimp fishermen drag their nets along the bottom of the sea. Several species of turtle get caught in the nets by mistake, including the Kemp's ridley turtle, which is the rarest species.

The nets used by fishermen can catch turtles by mistake. The turtles cannot escape, and they drown.

Pollution is a major threat to chelonians. Sea turtles often choke on plastic bags and toy balloons that float out to sea. The turtles confuse them with the jellyfish that they normally eat.

Oil pollution is also a serious threat to turtles. If oil is spilled on the water, turtles will take it into their bodies when they come to the surface to breathe. Often this means that the turtles will slowly die.

Turtles are among the many animals at risk from oil pollution from spills such as the Gulf oil slick.

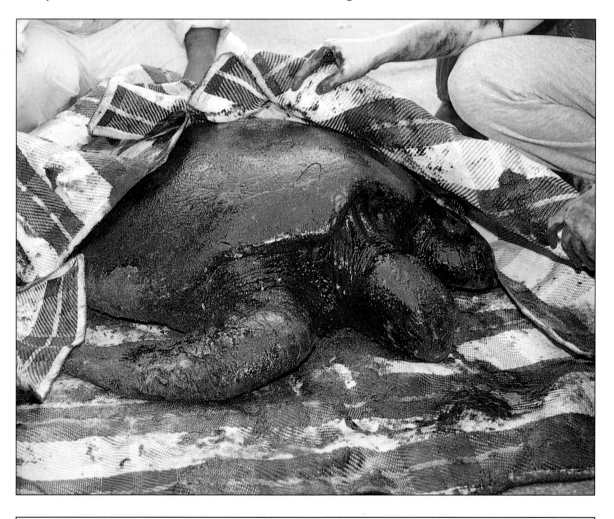

Tourism and turtles

Some of the places where turtles live are also popular areas for **tourism**. For instance, the popular Greek island of Zakynthos has more nesting turtles than anywhere else in the Mediterranean.

People can disturb the turtles in several ways. Turtles are easily frightened when they come onto the beach to lay their eggs. If tourists frighten turtles nesting on the beach, they may be forced to release their eggs into the sea where they are wasted. Cars being driven on the beach can crush buried eggs, and even beach umbrellas can spear eggs beneath the sand.

Cars that are driven on turtle beaches can destroy the nests.

These tourists must be careful not to disturb turtles that have made their nests on the Australian turtle beaches.

When the hatchlings are born they make their way to the sea by moving toward the dim light of the water. But the turtles can become confused by the lights of cafés and discos. If the hatchlings cannot find the sea before morning they are eaten by birds or other **predators**. In the sea, many turtles are injured by speedboats or get tangled in fishing nets.

In Terengganu, Malaysia, far too many tourists want to watch the leatherback turtles nesting.

Turtles are at risk from tourists in many countries. In the Mediterranean, turtles no longer nest on the beaches of Italy and Israel because they have been disturbed so much over the years. In Malaysia, at Terengganu, there are some very important nesting beaches. Thirty years ago, as many as two thousand leatherback turtles nested there every year. In 1989 only fifty animals nested.

Young turtles take thirty years to become adults. That means that if humans disturb the nesting turtles, it will be thirty years before we see the effects. By then there may be no young adults left to nest. In some parts of the world, like the Caribbean, there are already very few turtles left.

Pet turtles and tortoises

Many people want to have a pet turtle or tortoise of their own. Chelonians are very popular with children because of the Teenage Mutant Ninja Turtle craze. This means that animals like the red-eared terrapin and the American box turtle are sold in large numbers.

Every year as many as six million tortoises are collected from Morocco as pets. But it is now illegal to **import** some types of tortoises such as Mediterranean tortoises. However, these have been replaced by other species.

Many animals are very difficult to feed. Pet shops do not know the correct food for the more unusual animals. Also many countries are too cold to keep tortoises safely. Many suffer from diseases and die within a year.

Hermann's tortoise is still a very common pet. But it is now illegal to import this tortoise into some countries.

SAVING TURTLES AND TORTOISES

In order to save turtles and tortoises we must study them to find out the best ways of helping them. However, they are not easy animals to study. Some turtles and tortoises live much longer than the people trying to study them!

Sea turtles are difficult to study because they spend much of their lives at sea.

Scientists measure loggerhead turtles to see how fast they grow.

More turtle eggs hatch if scientists dig them up and re-bury them in protected areas.

Most of the studies on turtles have been done when the animals come on shore to lay their eggs. Scientists measure and tag some turtles. A tag is a label that identifies a particular turtle. Sometimes turtles that have been tagged in one place are later seen thousands of miles away. In this way we can find out more about turtle migration.

A scientist studying the tracks made by a hawksbill turtle.

Scientists on turtle beaches also study them by counting the number of tracks left by the turtles. This gives an idea of the number of animals that are nesting.

There are many species of tortoise that we know little about. It is important for scientists to study tortoises to find out how best to protect them.

Many countries are now taking action to save turtles and tortoises. In Mexico, the government has recently made a law that prevents anybody from killing turtles or taking their eggs. Before this law, more than 70,000 olive ridley turtles were killed in one year alone, for their skins. They were sold to Japan where their skins were made into expensive leather goods.

The Mexican beach where the Kemp's ridley turtle nests is now patrolled so no one can steal the eggs or harm the turtles. Some of the eggs are hatched in captivity. The hatchlings are kept for one year and then released in Texan waters. It is hoped they will begin to nest in these new areas.

The Kemp's ridley turtle is the rarest species of sea turtle.

Many loggerhead turtles nest on this beach in Dalyan in Turkey.

In the United States, shrimp fishermen now put a special kind of trap door into their nets to allow the turtles to escape. As a result, fewer Kemp's ridley turtles are being drowned.

In Turkey, large numbers of loggerhead turtles nest on the beaches of Dalyan.

Plans to build a big hotel have been stopped and three other nesting places have also been protected.

At last the Greek government has agreed that a nature reserve should be created on the island of Zakynthos to help save the remaining loggerhead turtles.

The rarest tortoise in the world is the plowshare tortoise, which lives only on Madagascar. There may be only a hundred left. The local people used to collect these tortoises and sell them to nearby islands as food. A new project has been set up to breed these tortoises in captivity to help save them. In the Galapagos Islands, giant tortoises are also bred in captivity to increase their numbers.

The Madagascan plowshare tortoise is the rarest tortoise and is found only in an area of 38 sq mi (100 sq km).

An international agreement called CITES (Convention on International Trade in Endangered Species) has restricted the trade in such species. However, some countries have still not agreed to this convention.

It is now illegal in most countries to import products made from endangered species such as turtles.

Although Japan has agreed, it still allows trade of some sea turtle meat and shells. Many hawskbill turtle shells are still sold to Japan, although in 1988 Japan banned the import of green turtle products.

If we are to save these ancient animals it is important to act now. Do not buy things made from turtles or tortoises. Take plastic bags and litter home from the beach. Do not let toy balloons drift away over the water. Tell your friends not to buy turtles or tortoises. If you are lucky enough to go to a turtle beach, be careful not to disturb the animals.

This beautiful tortoiseshell should stay where it belongs – on the back of its owner, the hawksbill turtle.

Glossary

Adapted   Changed to survive in different conditions.

Aquatic   Living in water.

Captivity   The state of being held in human care. A tortoise in a zoo is in captivity.

Chelonia   The group of animals consisting of turtles, tortoises and terrapins.

Coral reef   A solid structure formed by colonies of simple animals over thousands of years. Coral is found in warm waters and provides a home and food for many sea creatures.

Endangered   At risk of being wiped out.

Extinction   The dying out of a species. When there are no animals of a particular species left, the species is extinct.

Hatch   To break out of an egg.

Import   To bring in something from another country.

Mating   The joining together of a male and female to produce offspring.

Migration   The seasonal movement of animals from one part of the world to another.

Pollution   The harm caused to the natural environment when dangerous substances are released into it.

Predators   Animals that feed on other animals by hunting them.

Species   A group of animals that is different from all other groups. Only members of the same species can breed together.

Streamlined   Having a smooth, flowing shape that passes easily through air or water.

Ticks   Bloodsucking animals related to spiders.

Tortoiseshell   The thin outer layer of the shell of the hawksbill turtle. It is highly polished and used to make ornaments and jewelry.

Tourism   The industry of vacation travel.

Vegetarians   Animals that eat only plants and not other animals.

Further reading

Ancona, George. *Turtle Watch* (Macmillan, 1987*)*

Craig, Janet. *Turtles* (Troll Associates, 1982)

Fine, Edith H. *The Turtle and Tortoise* (Crestwood House, 1988)

Oda, Hidetomo. *The Turtle* (Raintree Publishers, 1986)

Serventy, Vincent. *Turtle and Tortoise* (Raintree Publishers, 1985)

Useful addresses

Conservation International Foundation
1015 18th Street NW
Washington D.C. 20036

Greenpeace USA
1436 U Street NW
Washington D.C. 20009

National Turtle and Tortoise Society
PO Box 9806
Phoenix, AZ 85068 9806

Index

Australia 8, 12, 21

Coral reefs 11
Crabs 10, 11

Eggs 6, 7, 9, 10, 18, 24, 26
Extinction 14, 15

Hatchlings 9, 10, 21, 26

Mating 6, 8
Mexico 8, 26
Migrations 10, 11, 24

Nesting beaches 9, 10, 11, 20, 22

Pollution 19

Scientists 24, 25
Sharks 10

Terrapins
  Diamondback 7, 12
  Red-eared 23
Tortoises
  Aldabran 7, 15
  Angulated 6
  Desert 4, 5
  Galapagos 7, 14, 15, 16, 28
  Hermann's 17
  Pancake 5, 7
  Plowshare 28
  Spur-thighed 17
Tortoiseshell 18

Turtles
  Box 13
  Green 9, 10, 11, 18, 21, 29
  Hawksbill 7, 11, 18, 25, 29
  Kemp's ridley 8, 18, 26, 27
  Leatherback 8, 11, 22
  Loggerhead 4, 8, 11, 24, 27
  Mata mata 12
  Olive ridley 8, 26
  Snake-necked 12
  Snapping 13

Picture acknowledgments

The photographs in this book were supplied by Oxford Scientific Films from the following photographers: Mike Birkhead 22; Tony Bomford 19; Mike Brown 10; W. Gregory Brown 11; Waina Cheng 29; John Cooke 9 (bottom), 13 (bottom); David Curl 6, 28 (top); Jack Dermid 24 (bottom); John Gerlach 4 (top); A. C. Highfield 16 (bottom), 17; Dean Lee 8, 21; Z. Leszczynski 7; C. C. Lockwood 18 (bottom), 24 (top); Godfrey Merlen 15; Stephen Mills 27; Patti Murray 12; Tsuneo Nakamura 16 (top); Richard Packwood *cover;* Vassili Papastavrou 18 (top), 20, 25; Hans Reinhard/Okapia 23; James H. Robinson 13 (top); Peter Ryley 14; Maurice Tibbles 9 (top); M. Wendler/Okapia 28 (bottom); Len Zell 4 (bottom). Planet Earth Pictures: Doug Perrine 26. Artwork is by Marilyn Clay.